English PUZZLES

3

DOUG CASE

HEINEMANN

Heinemann Games Series

Titles in this series include:

English Puzzles 1 Doug Case 0 435 28280 8
English Puzzles 2 Doug Case 0 435 28281 6
English Puzzles 3 Doug Case 0 435 28282 4
English Puzzles 4 Doug Case 0 435 28283 2

Play Games With English Book 1 Colin Granger 0 435 28060 0
Teacher's Book 1 0 435 28061 9
Play Games With English Book 2 Colin Granger 0 435 28062 7
Teacher's Book 2 0 435 28063 5

Word Games with English 1 Deirdre Howard-Williams & Cynthia Herd 0 435 28380 4
Word Games with English 2 Deirdre Howard-Williams & Cynthia Herd 0 435 28381 2
Word Games with English 3 Deirdre Howard-Williams & Cynthia Herd 0 435 28382 0
Word Games with English Plus Deirdre Howard-Williams & Cynthia Herd 0 435 28379 0

Heinemann International
A division of Heinemann Publishers (Oxford) Ltd
Halley Court, Jordan Hill, Oxford OX2 8EJ

OXFORD LONDON EDINBURGH MADRID PARIS ATHENS BOLOGNA
MELBOURNE SYDNEY AUCKLAND IBADAN NAIROBI GABORONE HARARE
PORTSMOUTH (NH) SINGAPORE TOKYO

ISBN 0 435 28282 4

© Doug Case 1991
First Published 1991

Acknowledgements
Thanks to Brigitte Zacharian for help in testing the puzzles in this
book, to Michèle Cronick and Charlotte Covill for deft and thoughtful
editing, and to them all for many valuable suggestions.

Illustrated by Nick Duffy, Belinda Evans, John Lobban and Laura Potter
Designed and typeset by Plum Design, Southampton
Printed and bound in Great Britain by Thomson Litho Ltd, East Kilbride, Scotland

92 93 94 95 96 10 9 8 7 6 5 4 3 2

Contents

Introduction

There are fifty puzzles in this book. They all help you to practise your English. This Introduction gives you some useful words. You often find these words in the instructions for English puzzles. (If you know Book 1 or Book 2 in this series, you already know most of these words.)

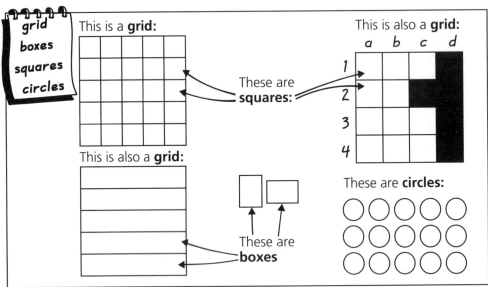

grid
boxes
squares
circles

This is a **grid:**

These are **squares:**

This is also a **grid:**

a b c d

1
2
3
4

This is also a **grid:**

These are **boxes**

These are **circles:**

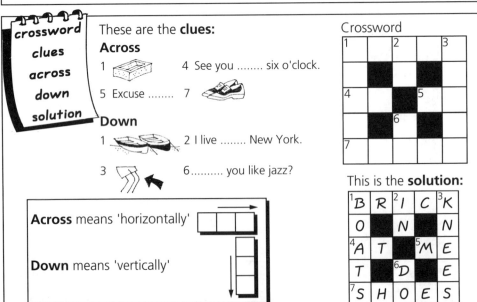

crossword
clues
across
down
solution

These are the **clues:**

Across

1 ◁ 4 See you .... six o'clock.

5 Excuse .... 7 👞

Down

1 🚣 2 I live .... New York.

3 👖 6 .... you like jazz?

Crossword

Across means 'horizontally'

Down means 'vertically'

This is the **solution:**

¹B	R	²I	C	³K
O		N		N
⁴A	T		⁵M	E
T		⁶D		E
⁷S	H	O	E	S

line
pair
group
spaces

This is a **line** of words:

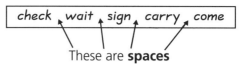

check · wait · sign · carry · come

These are **spaces**

This is a **pair** of symbols:

This is a **group** of pictures:

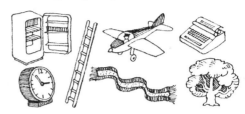

missing
the wrong order
the right order
code
anagram
riddle

This word is not complete. Two letters are **missing:**

| T | | W | | L |

(The missing letters are O and E. The complete word is TOWEL.)

In this word, the letters are in **the wrong order:**

| O | B | C | M |

(**The right order** – or the *correct* order – is C-O-M-B.)

This word is in **code:**

| 19 | 15 | 1 | 16 |

(The code is: 1=A, 15=O, 16=P, 19=S. So the word is SOAP.)

The word BREAD is an **anagram** of the word BEARD.

(Both words use the same letters.)

This is a **riddle** (a question which seems difficult to answer):

What can you put in your right hand but not in your left hand?

(The answer is: Your left elbow.)

complete
correct
circle
number
decode
fill in
cross out

Complete this film title:

'A [＿＿＿＿] AND A WOMAN'   'A MAN AND A WOMAN'

Correct the mistake:

 DANGIR

 DANGER

Circle the right picture:

SPOON

SPOON

Number these pictures:

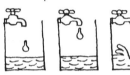

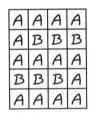
2   1   3

Decode this sign:

QSJWBUF   PRIVATE

(Q=P, S=R, J=I, etc.)

Fill in the A-squares:

Cross out the unnecessary
letters in this name:

ROBNERJT   ROBⁿERⱼT

A	A	A	A
A	B	B	B
A	A	A	A
B	B	B	A
A	A	A	A

Enjoy doing the puzzles – and remember:
when there are letters or numbers in a puzzle,
say them to yourself in *English*.

Use a *pencil,* in case you make a mistake!

You can find the *solutions* at the back of the book.

Down the steps

Make a sentence for each of the pictures. For each sentence, come down the steps, taking one word from each step.

Could	Could	Could	Could	Could	Could	Could
you	you	you	you	you	you	you
pass	wait	sign	carry	come	turn	cash
this	down	me	back	just	these	at
a	the	tomorrow	for	travellers	the	that
TV,	me,	moment,	cheques,	hammer,	morning,	bottom,
please?	please?	please?	please?	please?	please?	please?

Electrical appliances

Do you know the English words for these ten electrical appliances? Find the right plug for each one and it will give you the letters you need. Write the words in the grid.

Plugs:

| I P W / Y R E / E R T T | R C E / F A E F / O M K E | S A M H / N E W I G / C A N I H | M T / R C E / O U P | S T P S / E Y R L A / C E E A T |
| R A M / L N E E C / U C V A U | F G R O / I E R A / R E T R | N C I I S / G E W A N / A E M N H R | E E I O / D R E C / R R V O D | H S R / S I W / H E A D |

Grid:

	a	b	c	d	e	f	g	h	i	j	k	l	m	n	o	p	q
1	V	A	C	U	U	M	–	C	L	E	A	N	E	R			
2								–									
3																	
4																	
5																	
6								–									
7																	
8				–													
9								–									
10			–														

Find another electrical appliance by taking the correct letters from the grid.

9m	3k	5c	6j	1b	8a	7h		10c	2e	4g	1h		5d	1i	4f	6m	3g	9f

Unusual Activities

People sometimes do unusual things (to get into the 'Guinness Book of Records', for example): sitting in a cage full of spiders for three weeks, balancing a hundred plates one on top of another, etc.

Here are eight people, preparing to do unusual things. What is each person going to do?

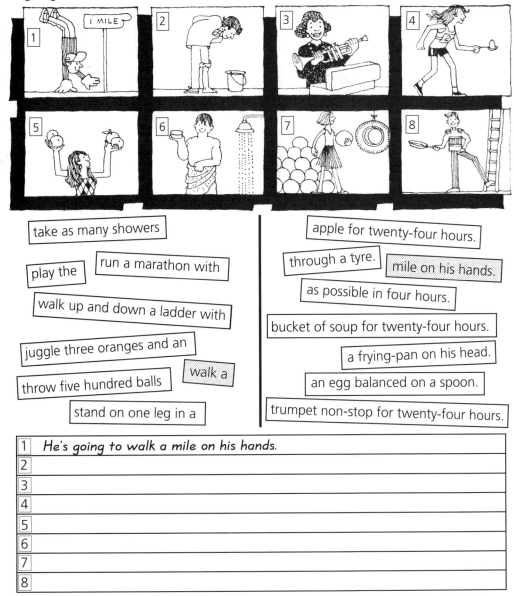

take as many showers	apple for twenty-four hours.

play the run a marathon with

walk up and down a ladder with

juggle three oranges and an

throw five hundred balls   walk a

stand on one leg in a

through a tyre.   mile on his hands.

as possible in four hours.

bucket of soup for twenty-four hours.

a frying-pan on his head.

an egg balanced on a spoon.

trumpet non-stop for twenty-four hours.

1	*He's going to walk a mile on his hands.*
2	
3	
4	
5	
6	
7	
8	

Find the beginnings

In each group in the grid, all three words need the same two letters at the beginning. Decide what the letters are, and write them in.

Then, for each group of words, find the correct group of pictures, and write the numbers in the correct boxes.

7	2 C H A I R			I R T		A M P
	3 C H E E S E			A T E		E A K
	1 C H U R C H			I E R		A R

O O N		I R T		A G
I D E R		O E S		U T E
I R A L		E E P		O W E R

O G		E A D		A Y
U I T		I C K		E E
I D G E		U S H		A I N

U M S		U G		O U D
E S S		A N T		O C K
A W E R		A T E		I F F

English Puzzles 3   Heinemann International

Rhyming pairs

Write the words with the pictures. (The words are in the box, but the letters are in the wrong order.)

Then put the words into rhyming pairs.   For example:

| ENEK |
| ULBL |
| YKE |
| HEQCEU |
| RMDU |
| YEE |
| IREF |
| AMEL |
| LATI |
| KECN |
| EPRA |
| KNESA |
| RASQEU |
| TESKA |
| MUHBT |
| ETI |
| YERT |
| HELAW |
| EWLEH |
| OWLO |

EYE	TIE

Sorry – I can explain!

Look at these two sentences (the first is in 'mirror-writing';
in the second, the spaces between the words are in the wrong places):

I'm sorry I'm late.

Myca rbro kedo wn.

In fact, those two sentences are an apology and an explanation:

I'm sorry I'm late.

My car broke down.

Here are ten more sentences – five apologies and five explanations.
Decode them and put each apology with the correct explanation.

1. I'm sorry I didn't phone you.

Itho ught itwa sthe seve ntee nth, n otth esev enth.

2. I'm sorry I didn't recognise you.

Thet ypew rite rbro kedo wn.

3. I'm sorry I forgot your birthday.

I'mno twea ring mygl asse s.

4. I'm sorry I didn't come to your party on Saturday.

llos tyou rnum ber.

5. I'm sorry I didn't finish typing your letters.

Iwas work inga llwe eken d.

APOLOGIES	EXPLANATIONS
1	
2	
3	
4	
5	

PARTS OF THE BODY

The parts of the body
in this picture all include the letter A.

1	A	R	M
2	E	A	R
3	H	A	N	D

Find the correct pictures for these other groups of words,
which include the letter E, the letter I, the letter O and the letter U.
Write the numbers in the pictures, and the words in the boxes.

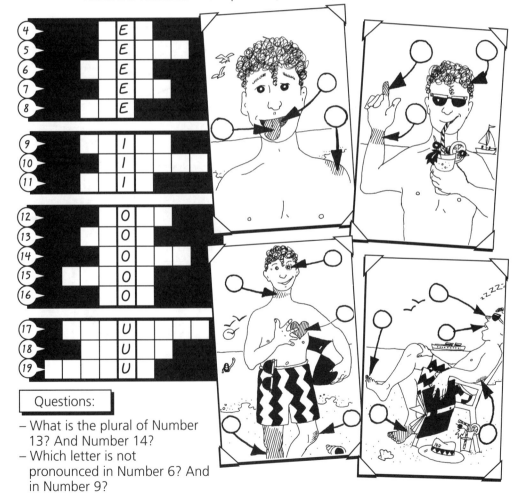

4	E
5	E
6	E
7	E
8	E

9	I
10	I
11	I

12	O
13	O
14	O
15	O
16	O

17	U
18	U
19	U

Questions:

- What is the plural of Number
  13? And Number 14?
- Which letter is not
  pronounced in Number 6? And
  in Number 9?

ELEPHANT JOKES

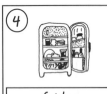

Elephant jokes are, of course, jokes about elephants –
usually a strange question and an amusing answer. Here
are seven of them. Join each question to the correct answer.

Questions

1 How does an elephant get down from a tree?

2 How do you put an elephant in a matchbox?

3 What time is it when an elephant sits on a chair?

4 How do you know if an elephant has been in your fridge?

5 Can an elephant jump higher than a lamp-post?

6 How do you get four elephants into a car?

7 How do you know if there's an elephant under your bed?

Answers

It's time to get a new chair.

You put two in the front and two in the back.

You can see footprints in the butter.

The ceiling is very close.

It sits on a leaf and waits for autumn.

Yes. Lamp-posts can't jump.

You take the matches out first.

These seven pictures show things mentioned in the jokes.
Write the numbers and the words.

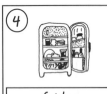

(4) fridge

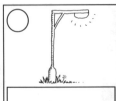

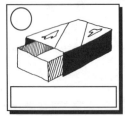

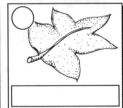

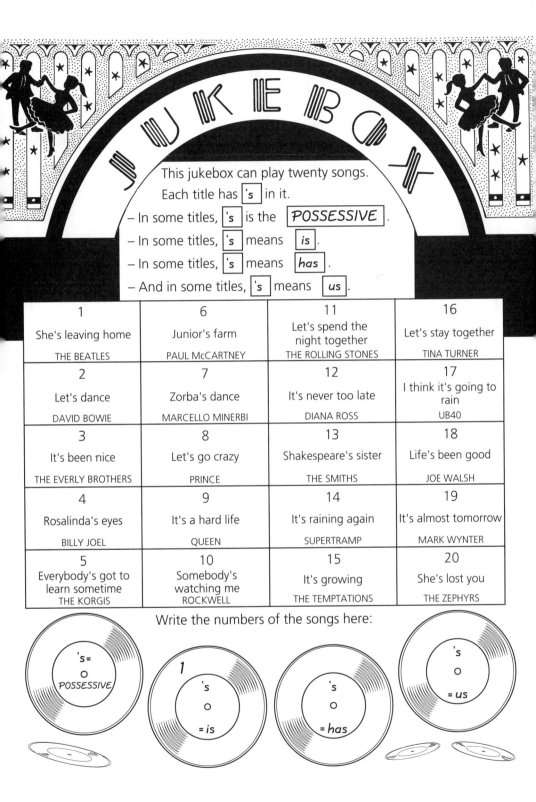

JUKEBOX

This jukebox can play twenty songs.
Each title has 's in it.
– In some titles, 's is the POSSESSIVE .
– In some titles, 's means is .
– In some titles, 's means has .
– And in some titles, 's means us .

1	6	11	16
She's leaving home	Junior's farm	Let's spend the night together	Let's stay together
THE BEATLES	PAUL McCARTNEY	THE ROLLING STONES	TINA TURNER
2	7	12	17
Let's dance	Zorba's dance	It's never too late	I think it's going to rain
DAVID BOWIE	MARCELLO MINERBI	DIANA ROSS	UB40
3	8	13	18
It's been nice	Let's go crazy	Shakespeare's sister	Life's been good
THE EVERLY BROTHERS	PRINCE	THE SMITHS	JOE WALSH
4	9	14	19
Rosalinda's eyes	It's a hard life	It's raining again	It's almost tomorrow
BILLY JOEL	QUEEN	SUPERTRAMP	MARK WYNTER
5	10	15	20
Everybody's got to learn sometime	Somebody's watching me	It's growing	She's lost you
THE KORGIS	ROCKWELL	THE TEMPTATIONS	THE ZEPHYRS

Write the numbers of the songs here:

's = POSSESSIVE

1 's = is

's = has

's = us

Who are the others ?

There are eight sentences in the grid, broken into parts.
Each sentence describes a famous man. The first
famous man – squares 1 and 14 – is Charles de Gaulle.
Who are the others?
(All the names are in the box, but the first part of each
name is not with the correct second part.)

A general. . . 1	An actor. . . 2	A secret agent. . . 3	A composer. . . 4
An artist. . . 5	A cowboy. . . 6	A detective. . . 7	A film-maker . . . 8
. . .who wrote nine symphonies . . . 9	. . .who was born in England 10	. . .whose number is 007. 11	. . .who is very intelligent. . . 12
. . .whose real name was William Cody. 13	. . .who became President of France. 14	. . .who invented Mickey Mouse. 15	. . .who painted the 'Mona Lisa' . . . 16
. . .and who has a friend called Dr Watson. 17	. . .and became famous in Hollywood. 18	. . .and was also a scientist. 19	. . .and who became deaf. 20

LEONARDO VAN BEETHOVEN
JAMES CHAPLIN
SHERLOCK DE GAULLE
WALT BILL
CHARLES DA VINCI
BUFFALO BOND
LUDWIG DISNEY
CHARLIE HOLMES

one	fourteen		1	14	CHARLES DE GAULLE
two	ten	eighteen			
three	eleven				
four	nine	twenty			
five	sixteen	nineteen			
six	thirteen				
seven	twelve	seventeen			
eight	fifteen				

Question: Which two of those famous men are not real people?

English Puzzles 3   Heinemann International

Verb flags

Each flag shows the Base Form and the *Past Simple* form of a verb. Add the third form, the Past Participle, for each one, and then answer the questions.

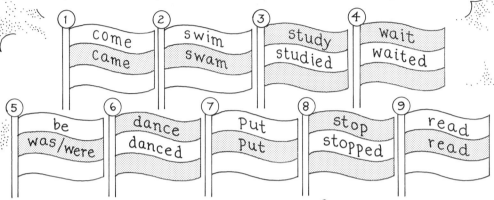

Questions:

● Why are some of the flags like this 🏳 and some like this 🏳 ?

● Which of the ten verbs does each of these sentences describe? Add the correct numbers.

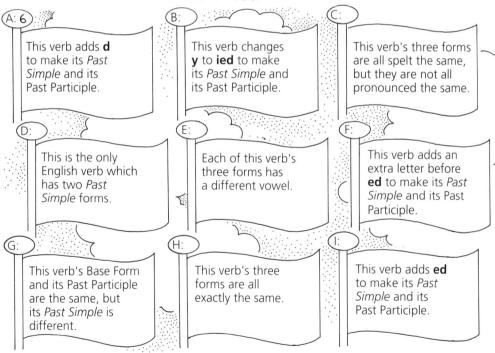

A: 6
This verb adds **d** to make its *Past Simple* and its Past Participle.

B:
This verb changes **y** to **ied** to make its *Past Simple* and its Past Participle.

C:
This verb's three forms are all spelt the same, but they are not all pronounced the same.

D:
This is the only English verb which has two *Past Simple* forms.

E:
Each of this verb's three forms has a different vowel.

F:
This verb adds an extra letter before **ed** to make its *Past Simple* and its Past Participle.

G:
This verb's Base Form and its Past Participle are the same, but its *Past Simple* is different.

H:
This verb's three forms are all exactly the same.

I:
This verb adds **ed** to make its *Past Simple* and its Past Participle.

Eight proverbs

Here are eight English proverbs.
In three of them, you have to put the word *the* in each space: THE ✎ THE ✎ ....

In five of them, each space must have nothing in it: ▮ ✎ ▮ ✎ ....

▮ TIME IS ▮ MONEY .

☐ WALLS HAVE ☐ EARS .

☐ FIRST STEP IS ☐ HARDEST .

☐ SLEEP IS BETTER THAN ☐ MEDICINE .

☐ PEOPLE WHO LIVE IN ☐ GLASS HOUSES SHOULDN'T
THROW ☐ STONES .

☐ GRASS IS ALWAYS GREENER ON ☐ OTHER SIDE
OF ☐ FENCE .

WHEN ☐ CAT'S AWAY , ☐ MICE WILL PLAY .

WHILE THERE'S ☐ LIFE , THERE'S ☐ HOPE .

Write the correct proverb under each picture.

PUZZLE 12

Album TRACKS

A piece of music on an album is called a *track*. So an album could have ten *tracks* on it, for example.

Here are the titles of the tracks on Michael Jackson's album 'Bad', in alphabetical order:

Another part of me   Bad   Dirty Diana   I just can't stop loving you

Just good friends   Liberian girl   Man in the mirror   Smooth criminal

Speed demon   The way you make me feel

Using the clues, write the titles of the tracks in the correct places on the two sides of the album.

Clues

In the title of *Side B Track 2,* half the words begin with the same letter.

The title of *Side A Track 4* includes an adjective of nationality.

The title of *Side B Track 5* has two words, and the second word is longer than the first word.

The title of *Side A Track 2* has nineteen letters.

In the title of *Side B Track 4,* both words begin with the same letter, and one of the words is a girl's name.

The title of *Side A Track 1* is just one word (an adjective).

The title of *Side A Track 5* includes a plural noun.

The title of *Side B Track 1* includes the word *me,* but not the word *you.*

The title of *Side B Track 3* includes the word *you,* but not the word *me.*

In the title of *Side A Track 3,* the last letter of the first word is the same as the first letter of the last word.

SIDE A

1 _____
2 _____
3 _____
4 _____
5 _____

SIDE B

1 _____
2 _____
3 _____
4 _____
5 _____

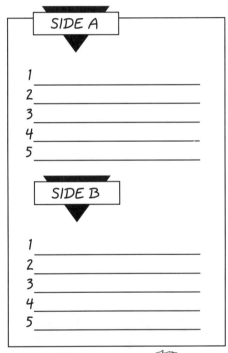

From dinosaurs to dynamite

Put the correct letter beside each sentence.

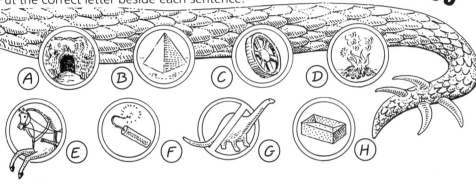

1. (G) The dinosaurs disappeared about 65,000,000 years ago.
2. ( ) Fire was used for the first time about 500,000 years ago.
3. ( ) Caves were used as homes in Europe about 150,000 years ago.
4. ( ) The first brick houses were built about 7,500 years ago.
5. ( ) The first vehicles with wheels were used about 5,500 years ago.
6. ( ) The first pyramid in Egypt was built about 4,700 years ago.
7. ( ) Horses were first used to pull vehicles about 3,800 years ago.
8. ( ) Alfred Nobel invented dynamite about 100 years ago.

The numbers from the sentences are in this grid, written in words. Put the correct letters in the circles.

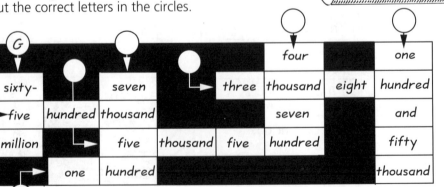

Complete the jokes

In this puzzle, there are six jokes. They are all conversations between a teacher, *T*, and a student, *S*.
Complete each joke by putting in the four missing words and the missing punchline.
(A 'punchline' is the last line of a joke.)

Missing words

dollars	baby	hand	and		trousers	rabbits
jacket	said	left	difference		pocket	many
another	plural	oranges	hamburgers		apples	tomorrow
pocket	if	ten	eighty		would	five

Missing punchlines

Yes. I've already got one at home.

Very big hands.

Twins.

Yes, but I don't like hamburgers.

Very heavy trousers.

Someone else's jacket.

(1)

T If I had eight oranges in my right hand and .*ten oranges* in my *left hand*, what would I have?
S *Very big hands.*

(2)

T If you had fifty dollars in one jacket-pocket and a hundred .... in ....- ...., what would you have?
S ....

(3)

T If I offered you eight hamburgers or ...., which would you prefer?
S Eight.
T Eight? Don't you know the . ... between eight .... eighty?
S ....

(4)

T If I had ten .... in each .... of my ...., what .... I have?
S ....

(5)

T If I gave you three rabbits today and ...., how .... rabbits would you have?
S Nine.
T Nine?
S ....

(6)

T If I said 'What is the plural of "mouse"?', what would you say?
S Mice.
T And .... I .... 'What is the .... of "....................."?', what would you say?
S ....

English Puzzles 3   Heinemann International

PUZZLE 15

N,S,E,W

First, discover why these four words have
been placed in different sections of the compass.
(Look very carefully at the letters in each word.)

 PANDA

 RUNWAY

 SHIP

 CASE

Then write the words
for the other sixteen
things in the correct
sections. (If you're not
sure of some of the
words, you can find
them all at the bottom
of the page.) When
you've finished, there
should be at least one
word in each section.

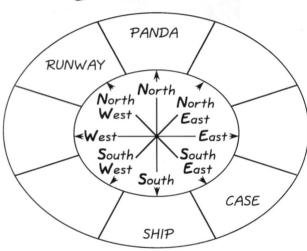

NECK NET PAINT SCARF SWITCH TOURIST WATCH WOOD

BALCONY CAMERA COMPUTER COW HORSE LADDER LIPSTICK MUSEUM

Five pockets

What has this man got in his pockets? Put the letters for each thing in the correct order, and write the words in the correct boxes. (All the things appear in the picture at the bottom of the page.)

In the front pocket of his jeans, he's got his ACR-EKSY and his EHOSU-EKSY.

In the back pocket of his jeans, he's got a ACDEEFHHIKNR.

In the inside pocket of his jacket, he's got his AELLTW, his CEEHQU-BKOO, his DGIINRV-CCEEILN and his CDEIRT-ACDRS.

In the top pocket of his jacket, he's got some ENPS and a AGHHOOPPRT of his family.

In the other pocket of his jacket, he's got a BCMO and his AEGLSSS.

CAR-KEYS

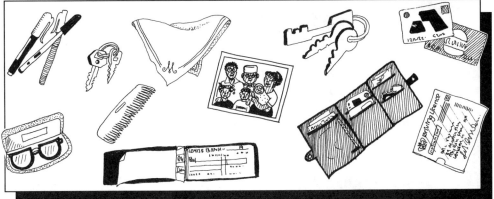

It doesn't rhyme!

For this crossword, the clues are groups of words. In each group of three words, find the one which does not rhyme with the other two. Put that word into the grid.

English Puzzles 3   Heinemann International

REVEAL THE ANSWERS

Look at these crossword clues:

Across

Our team played very (bad).

Down

Their team played very (good).

The answers are in this grid:

T	E	R	W	I
N	L	P	E	H
B	A	D	L	Y
O	M	S	L	E

Here they are:

T	E	R	W	I
N	L	P	E	H
B	A	D	L	Y
O	M	S	L	E

Reveal the answers to these clues...

▶**Across**

...in this grid.

Could you speak (slow), please?

Drive (careful)!

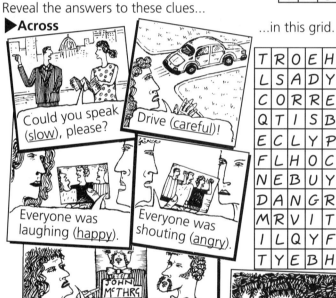

T	R	O	E	H	A	P	P	I	L	Y	I	G	N
L	S	A	D	Y	I	C	O	H	R	D	L	E	P
C	O	R	R	E	C	T	L	Y	U	G	E	N	L
Q	T	I	S	B	A	F	I	D	E	K	C	T	O
E	C	L	Y	P	E	X	T	A	Q	I	O	L	M
F	L	H	O	C	A	R	E	F	U	L	L	Y	R
N	E	B	U	Y	S	A	L	M	I	T	V	E	C
D	A	N	G	R	I	L	Y	O	C	L	N	Y	E
M	R	V	I	T	L	E	B	Y	K	S	A	N	W
I	L	Q	Y	F	Y	A	N	S	L	O	W	L	Y
T	Y	E	B	H	L	O	V	C	Y	A	R	I	H

Everyone was laughing (happy).

Everyone was shouting (angry).

Have I spelt your name (correct)?

This plant grows very (quick), doesn't it?

Speak to him very (polite).

▼**Down**

I think I'll win quite (easy).

Push it (gentle)!

I can't see very (clear).

English Puzzles 3   Heinemann International

Riddles

A *riddle* is a question that seems difficult to answer. The answer is usually clever or amusing. For example:

Q: What has a hundred legs but can't walk?
A: Fifty pairs of trousers.

Here are the answers to eight more riddles. Put them with the correct questions.

A blackboard.	A comb.	A hot dog.	A hole.
A mushroom.	A stamp.	A telephone.	Rain.

1. Q: What can get bigger without getting heavier?
   A:

2. Q: What travels round the world but always stays in the same corner?
   A:

3. Q: What is black when it's clean and white when it's dirty?
   A:

4. Q: What falls but never gets hurt?
   A:

5. Q: What doesn't ask questions but often needs to be answered?
   A:

6. Q: What has teeth but can't bite?
   A:

7. Q: What kind of dog has no tail?
   A:

8. Q: What kind of room has no walls, no floor and no ceiling?
   A:

English Puzzles 3   Heinemann International

Guitar chords

These diagrams represent seven guitar chords. (If you don't play the guitar, don't worry – you can still do the puzzle.)

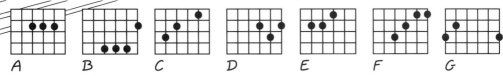

In the crossword clues, the diagrams give you some of the letters of the answers. Find the other letters in the box. All the answers are types of music.

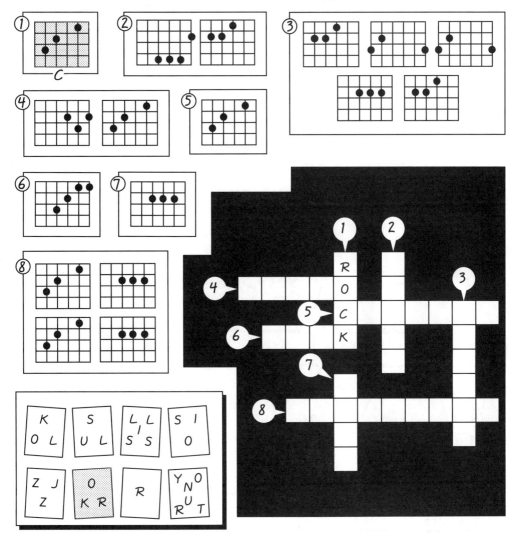

Looking into the future

In 1973, Margaret Thatcher made a prediction. She said this:

I do not think a woman will be the British Prime Minister in my lifetime.

MARGARET THATCHER, politician, 1973

Her prediction was wrong. She became Prime Minister herself in 1979.

Here are six more predictions. Like Margaret Thatcher's, they were all wrong. Put in the missing words – two in each prediction. (All the words you need are in the box.)

do | never | two
end | popular | war
impossible | president | world
moon | twentieth | year

1 We will go to the ⬭.

SIR HAROLD SPENCER JONES, British astronomer, 1957

2 In the ⬭ century, ⬭ will not exist.

VICTOR HUGO, French writer, 1842

3 The Rolling Stones will only be ⬭ for ⬭ years.

MICK JAGGER, singer, 1964

4 They will never ⬭ it. It's ⬭.

The WRIGHT BROTHERS' father, before their first flight, 1903

5 Fidel Castro will not be ⬭ for more than a ⬭.

FULGENCIO BATISTA, ex-president of Cuba, 1959

6 The ⬭ will ⬭ on 20th February, 1524.

JOHANNES STOEFTLER, German astrologer, Jan.1524

First, put the letters of these words in the correct order.

(1) D A R B E / B R E A D

(2) F E C F E O

(3) Y L F

(4) C I E - E M C A R

(5) I K M L

(6) Z I A P Z

(7) O P S A

(8) O S P U

(9) R P D S E I

(10) A T E

(11) U B T M H

Now look at these restaurant jokes. In each joke, a customer says something and a waiter answers. Put in the missing words, and then assemble the jokes.

Customer

Waiter! There's a (3) _fly_ in my (8) _soup_ !

Waiter! What's this (3) _____ doing in my (8) _____ ?

Waiter! What's this (3) _____ doing on my (4) _____ ?

Waiter! Your (11) _____ is in my (8) _____ !

Waiter! I'll have (2) _____ without (5) _____ , please.

Waiter! This (2) _____ tastes like (7) _____ !

Waiter! How long will my (6) _____ be?

Waiter

I think it's learning to ski, sir.

We haven't got any (5) _____ , sir. Would you like (2) _____ without cream?

I think it's swimming, sir.

It won't be _long_, sir. It'll be _round_.

Don't worry, sir. The (9) _spider_ on your (1) _bread_ will kill it.

Ah, that must be (10) _____ , sir. The (2) _____ tastes like glue.

Don't worry, sir. It's not very hot.

Words into numbers

In this puzzle, the clues are the areas of countries (in square kilometres).
Read the words and put the numbers into the grid.

▶ Across

B *Greenland*: Two million, one hundred and seventy-five thousand, six hundred.
F *Brunei*: Five thousand, seven hundred and sixty-five.
G *Martinique*: One thousand, one hundred.
I *Namibia*: Eight hundred and twenty-four thousand.
L *Togo*: Fifty-six thousand, seven hundred.
N *Bahrain*: Six hundred.
O *Liechtenstein*: One hundred and sixty.
P *Albania*: Twenty-eight thousand, five hundred.
R *The Netherlands*: Forty-one thousand, three hundred.
S *Barbados*: Four hundred and thirty.

▼ Down

A *The USA*: Nine million, three hundred and sixty-three thousand, four hundred and five.
C *Gambia*: Eleven thousand, one hundred.
D *Guam*: Five hundred and forty.
E *China*: Nine million, five hundred and fifty-eight thousand.
H *Australia*: Seven million, six hundred and eighty-seven thousand.
J *Malta*: Three hundred and sixteen.
K *Italy*: Three hundred and one thousand, two hundred and twenty-five.
M *Sierra Leone*: Seventy-two thousand.
O *Montserrat*: One hundred and three.
Q *Singapore*: Five hundred and eighty-four.

At the cinema

Imagine that A and B are pieces of glass. If you placed one on top of the other, you could read the words SPY FILM.

A ⟩ ⟩

B ⟩ ⟩ → SPY FILM

Do the same with these other 'pieces of glass', and you will find six more types of film. Write them under the correct pictures.

Heavy syllables

Read these words aloud:

 MONUMENT  CATHEDRAL

Both words have three syllables (MON/U/MENT, CA/THE/DRAL), but the *stress* is different.

In **MONUMENT**, the stress is on the first syllable: the first syllable is 'heavier' than the other two.

In **CATHEDRAL**, the stress is on the second syllable: the second syllable is 'heavier' than the other two.

Here are sixteen more words. Write them on the correct groups of weights.

There are eight like this: and eight like this:

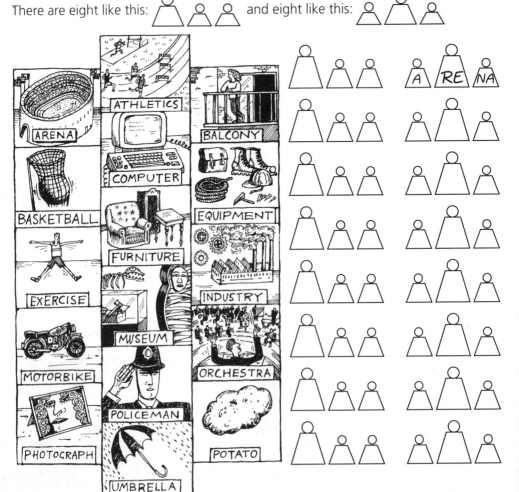

Special sentences

Look at this sentence:

Has everybody left London, Oliver?

It is special, because if you take the first letter of each word, you find: *Hello*.

In the pictures below, there are nine more sentences. Discover why each one is special. The reasons are given in this box:

Write the numbers of the sentences here.

In Sentence ☐ , all the words except one include double letters.
In Sentence ☐ , four words begin with the same letter.
In Sentence ☐ , all the words have the same number of letters.
In Sentence ☐ , all the words begin with the same letter.
In Sentence ☐ , the second word has one more letter than the first word, the third word has one more letter than the second word, and so on.
In Sentence ☐ , only one word includes the letter *e*.
In Sentence ☐ , there is a consonant, then a vowel, then a consonant, then a vowel, and so on.
In Sentence ☐ , three words include the letter *v*.
In Sentence ☐ , the letters are an anagram of *Warm feet, Beethoven?*

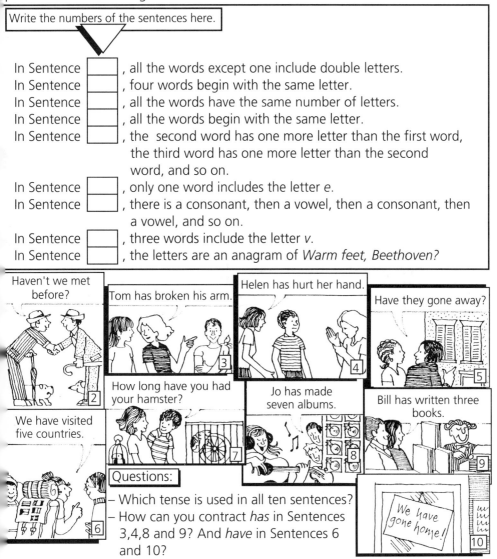

Haven't we met before?

Tom has broken his arm.

Helen has hurt her hand.

Have they gone away?

How long have you had your hamster?

Jo has made seven albums.

Bill has written three books.

We have visited five countries.

Questions:
– Which tense is used in all ten sentences?
– How can you contract *has* in Sentences 3,4,8 and 9? And *have* in Sentences 6 and 10?

We have gone home!

Find the middles

In each group in the grid, all three words need the same two (or three) letters in the middle. Decide what the letters are, and write them in.
Then, for each group of words, find the correct group of pictures, and write the numbers in the correct boxes.

5	2	S	A	L	T
	1	B	A	L	L
	3	H	A	L	F

	B	U			E	R
	B	O			L	E
	L	E			E	R

	H					Y
	C					S
	M					Y

	D				R
	P				L
	F				T

	B	U			E	R
	M	A			E	S
	K	I			E	N

	N			L
	H			R
	R			N

	E				T
	L				T
	N				T

	C	O			A	R
	W	A			E	T
	P	I			O	W

	F			E
	G			L
	B			D

Doctor!

The last line of a joke is called the *punchline*. Find the correct punchline for each of these jokes. (All of the jokes are conversations between a doctor, *D*, and a patient, *P*.)

1
P Doctor, I've swallowed a pencil. What shall I do?
D *Use a pen.*

2
P Doctor, I've lost my memory.
D When did this happen?
P

3
P Good morning, doctor.
D Good morning, Mr Jones. I haven't seen you for a long time.
P

4
P What do you think, doctor?
D Have you had this problem before?
P Yes, doctor.
D

5
P Doctor, I'm very nervous. This is the first operation I've ever had.
D

6
P Doctor , I think I've become invisible.
D

7
P Doctor, after the operation, will I be able to play the violin?
D Yes, of course.
P

8
P Doctor, no-one is interested in me.
D

Punchlines

That's fantastic! I've never been able to play it before.

I'm nervous too. It's the first operation I've ever done.

Well, you've got it again.

I know, doctor. I've been ill.

Who said that?

Next!

1 Use a pen.

When did <u>what</u> happen?

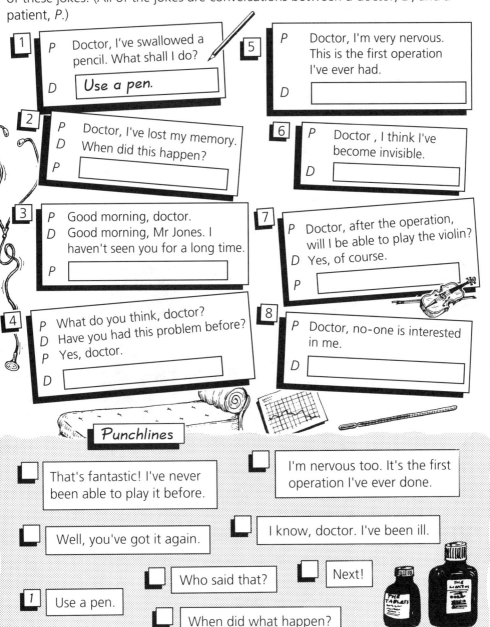

NUMBERPLATES

Do you know the English words for the car parts marked in the pictures?
The numberplates will help you: each numberplate includes the first letter
and the last three letters of the word you need. For example, the first
answer is MIRROR (the numberplate includes the letters M and ROR).

Absurd riddles

There is a particular kind of riddle which we can call an 'absurd riddle'.
Its answer is logical but silly (or 'absurd'). Here are two examples:

What is yellow and always points
to the north? – A magnetic banana.

What is white and yellow and
travels at 200 kilometres an hour?
– A train-driver's egg sandwich.

Here are eight more absurd riddles.
Complete the answers with the help of the pictures.
(All the words you need are at the bottom of the page.)

1. What is red and goes up
   and down?
   A __tomato__ in a __lift__ .

2. What has six legs, four
   ears and a tail?
   A _____ on a _____ .

3. What is soft and yellow and
   goes round and round?
   An _____ in a _____ .

4. What is black and white
   and has eight wheels?
   A _____ on _____ .

5. What is black and white, has four
   legs and makes a lot of noise?
   A _____ with a _____ .

6. What can fly underwater?
   A _____ in a _____ .

7. What has big ears and can travel at
   150 kilometres an hour underground?
   A _____ on a _____ .

8. What is very tall and
   has a very loud voice?
   A _____ with a _____ .

One more question:

What is big and yellow
and eats rocks?

zebra
washing-machine
trumpet tomato submarine rollerskates
rabbit penguin omelette motorbike
microphone man lift horse bird giraffe

Crossword in two halves

This crossword is about verbs. Each clue gives you the Base Form and the *Past Simple* form of a verb – and the Past Participle is missing. For each verb, decide what the Past Participle is, and put it into the grid.

Across

2 GIVE / GAVE
3 MEET / MET
5 STAND / STOOD
7 WRITE / WROTE
10 FIND / FOUND
11 LEAVE / LEFT
12 SING / SANG
13 THINK / THOUGHT
14 EAT / ATE

Down

1 SAY / SAID
2 GO / WENT
4 TEACH / TAUGHT
5 SLEEP / SLEPT
6 DRINK / DRANK
8 TAKE / TOOK
9 SEE / SAW

Part A   **Part B**

Question:

The crossword is divided into two halves. Can you think of a reason why the verbs in Part A are different from the verbs in Part B? (Look carefully at their *Past Simple* forms and their Past Participles.)

Film encyclopedia

Look at this extract from the index to a film encyclopedia.
(It is an encyclopedia of films from the United States and the United Kingdom.)

THE MAN FROM LARAMIE	US, 1955
THE MAN FROM PLANET X	US, 1951
THE MAN IN GREY	UK, 1943
THE MAN IN THE BACK SEAT	UK, 1961
THE MAN IN THE IRON MASK	US, 1939
THE MAN IN THE WHITE SUIT	UK, 1951
THE MAN ON THE EIFFEL TOWER	US, 1948
THE MAN UPSTAIRS	UK, 1958
THE MAN WHO CAME BACK	US, 1930
THE MAN WHO CAME TO DINNER	US, 1941
THE MAN WHO FELL TO EARTH	UK, 1976
THE MAN WHO LOVED WOMEN	US, 1983
THE MAN WHO SHOT LIBERTY VALANCE	US, 1962
THE MAN WHO TALKED TOO MUCH	US, 1940
THE MAN WHO WATCHED TRAINS GO BY	UK, 1952
THE MAN WITH THE GOLDEN GUN	UK, 1974
THE MAN WITH TWO FACES	US, 1934

These are posters for eight of the films.
Write the correct title on each poster.

Question: In these four titles, a word is hidden – the same word in each title.
What is the word?

THE BOY	STOLE A MILLION	UK, 1960
THE GIRL	HAD EVERYTHING	US, 1953
THE SPY	LOVED ME	UK, 1977
THE WOMAN	CAME BACK	US, 1945

Silent letters

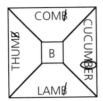

Look at this group of four words:

```
        COMB
THUMB  [ B ]  CUCUMBER
        LAMB
```

The letter B is only pronounced in one word: CUCUMBER.
In the other three words, the letter B is silent:
COMB, LAMB, THUMB.

Mark the words in these groups in the same way. In each group:

- *circle* the letter in the word in which it is pronounced.

- *cross out* the letter in the three words in which it is silent.

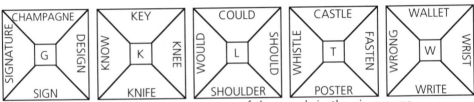

```
         CHAMPAGNE          KEY            COULD           CASTLE          WALLET
SIGNATURE  [ G ]  DESIGN  KNOW [K] KNEE  WOULD [L] SHOULD  WHISTLE [T] FASTEN  WRONG [W] WRIST
           SIGN            KNIFE          SHOULDER         POSTER          WRITE
```

These pictures represent some of the words in the six groups.
For each one, write the correct letter in the square.

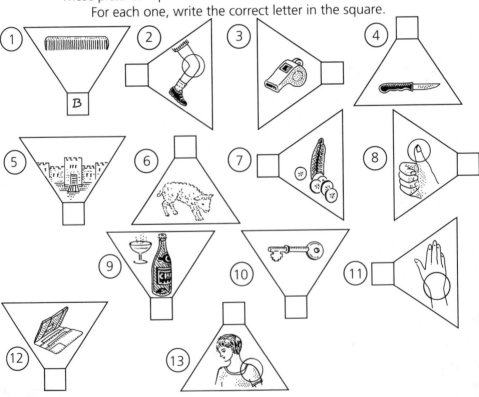

English Puzzles 3   Heinemann Internation

Football team

Each member of this football team is saying something false.
Write the contradictions to Numbers 2–11 in the grid. In the diagonal line of squares, you should find the contradiction to what the goalkeeper is saying.

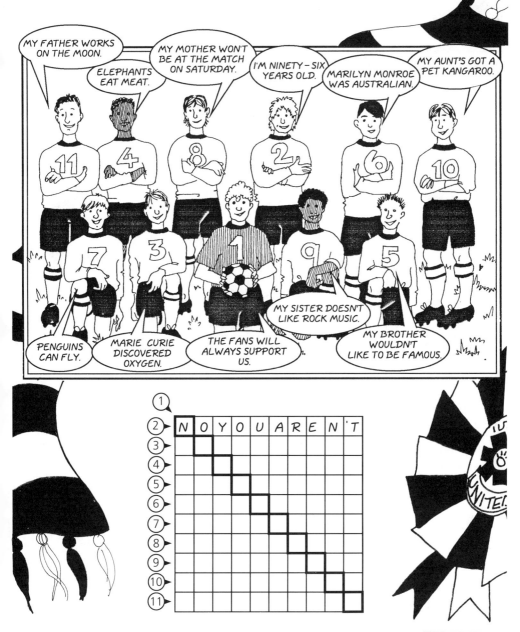

Personality

These playing cards represent the letters of the alphabet. As you can see, two cards can represent the same letter.

A ♦	2 ♦	3 ♦	4 ♦	5 ♦	6 ♦	7 ♦	8 ♦	9 ♦	10 ♦	J ♦	Q ♦	K ♦

A ♥	2 ♥	3 ♥	4 ♥	5 ♥	6 ♥	7 ♥	8 ♥	9 ♥	10 ♥	J ♥	Q ♥	K ♥

(a)(b)(c)(d)(e)(f)(g)(h)(i)(j)(k)(l)(m)   (n)(o)(p)(q)(r)(s)(t)(u)(v)(w)(x)(y)(z)

A ♣	2 ♣	3 ♣	4 ♣	5 ♣	6 ♣	7 ♣	8 ♣	9 ♣	10 ♣	J ♣	Q ♣	K ♣

A ♠	2 ♠	3 ♠	4 ♠	5 ♠	6 ♠	7 ♠	8 ♠	9 ♠	10 ♠	J ♠	Q ♠	K ♠

Discover the personality of each of these people from the cards they are holding.

① L A Z Y

② ☐☐☐☐☐☐☐

③ ☐☐☐☐☐

④ ☐☐☐☐☐☐☐

⑤ ☐☐☐☐ – ☐☐☐☐☐☐

⑥ ☐☐☐☐☐☐

⑦ ☐☐☐☐☐☐☐☐

⑧ ☐☐☐☐☐ – ☐☐☐☐

Question: Why are the eight people in two groups of four?

English Puzzles 3   Heinemann International

◁▯Past, present and future ▯▷

The clues in this puzzle are questions – about the past, the present and the future. Read the questions carefully, and write the answers in the grid. (The answers are *days* and *months*.)

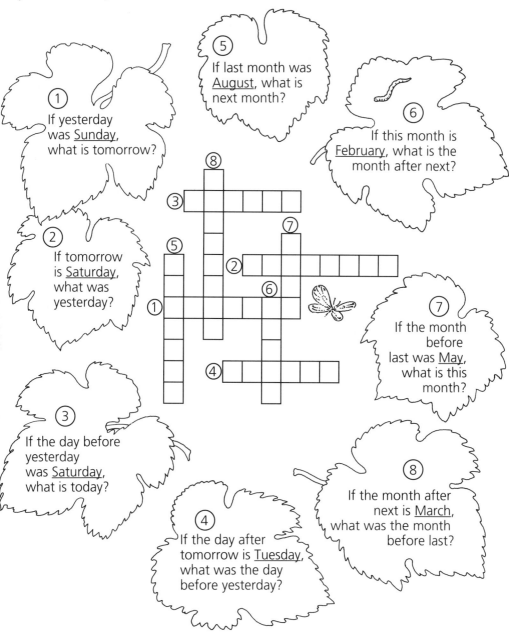

⑤ If last month was <u>August</u>, what is next month?

① If yesterday was <u>Sunday</u>, what is tomorrow?

⑥ If this month is <u>February</u>, what is the month after next?

② If tomorrow is <u>Saturday</u>, what was yesterday?

⑦ If the month before last was <u>May</u>, what is this month?

③ If the day before yesterday was <u>Saturday</u>, what is today?

⑧ If the month after next is <u>March</u>, what was the month before last?

④ If the day after tomorrow is <u>Tuesday</u>, what was the day before yesterday?

A Strange quiz

The questions and answers in this quiz are strange, but they are logical.
Find the correct answers in the boxes, and write them under the questions.

1. Which part of London is in Brazil?
   _____

2. Why shouldn't you put the letter M into a refrigerator?
   _____

3. Which question always has the answer 'Yes'?
   _____

4. Which question can never have the answer 'Yes'?
   _____

5. What is the longest word in the English language?
   _____

6. Which English word is always pronounced wrongly?
   _____

7. Which five-letter word has six left when you take two letters away?
   _____

8. What can you always find in the middle of March?
   _____

9. What can you find once in every <u>minute</u>, but never in <u>a thousand years</u>?
   _____

10. What starts with a P, ends with an E, and has thousands of letters?
    _____

11. Why is the letter B hot?
    _____

12. Why is the letter E lazy?
    _____

13. Why is the letter T like an island?
    _____

The letter R.

Post office.

Because it makes oil boil.

Because it changes ice into mice.

Smiles (because there is a mile between the first letter and the last letter).

Are you asleep?

How do you pronounce 'y - e - s'?

Sixty.

Because it's in the middle of water.

The letter L.

Because it's always in bed.

The letters M and I.

The word that's spelt w - r - o - n - g - l - y.

Which routes?

As you can see on the street-plan, these directions:

> Go north past the supermarket, take
> the second right, and go straight on.

describe this route: (G) → (D)

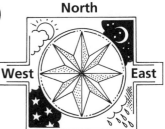

North

West ← ◆ → **East**

South

(A)

DISCO

(B)

SCH
SCHOOL

(C)

POST OFFICE

(J)

BOOKSHOP

GARAGE
BANK

LIBRARY

(D)

CINEMA

(I)

CHURCH

SUPERMARKET

(E)

(H)   (G)   (F)

Which routes do these directions describe?

1	Go south past the post office. When you see a cinema on a corner, turn left.	◯ → ◯
2	Go east past the bookshop, take the first right, then the first left, then the first right.	◯ → ◯
3	Go north and turn right at the church. Then turn left at the bank, turn right at the library and go straight on.	◯ → ◯
4	Go south past one set of traffic lights, then straight on past another set of traffic lights, and straight on again.	◯ → ◯
5	Go west. When you get to a garage on a corner, turn right. Then take the first left.	◯ → ◯
6	Go south past the disco and turn left at the school. Then take the first right and go straight on.	◯ → ◯

DEPARTMENT STORE

In this department store guide, some of the letters are missing – ■ – and the others are in Morse Code. Can you work out what the departments are?

Morse Code

A	•−	N	−•
B	−•••	O	−−−
C	−•−•	P	•−−•
D	−••	Q	−−•−
E	•	R	•−•
F	••−•	S	•••
G	−−•	T	−
H	••••	U	••−
I	••	V	•••−
J	•−−−	W	•−−
K	−•−	X	−••−
L	•−••	Y	−•−−
M	−−	Z	−−••

Write the names of the departments here:

Ground floor
1
2
3
4

First floor
1
2
3

Second floor
1
2
3

English Puzzles 3   Heinemann Internation

Missing words

First, decide if the missing word in each sentence is *since* or *for*.

They've been married _for_ forty years. | 13 30

We've only lived in this house ____ a week. | 5 33

I've been here ____ six o'clock. | 2 27

We've known each other ____ ages! | 9 24

Zambia has been independent ____ 1964. | 8 20

I've had this car ____ twenty-five years. | 3 28

We've been away ____ six months. | 11 26

I've been here ____ twenty minutes. | 7 32

He's been interested in horses ____ he was a boy. | 21 29

She's worked in this office ____ thirty years. | 1 22

Now look at the numbers under the pictures in which you wrote *for*. Fill in the letters below which have those numbers, and the name of a tense will appear.

Trick Questions

A 'trick question' seems easy to answer, but it isn't. Look at this conversation:

Which month has 28 days?

February.

No! _All_ the months have 28 days! It was a trick question!

Assemble four more conversations like that – taking an A, then a B, then a C:

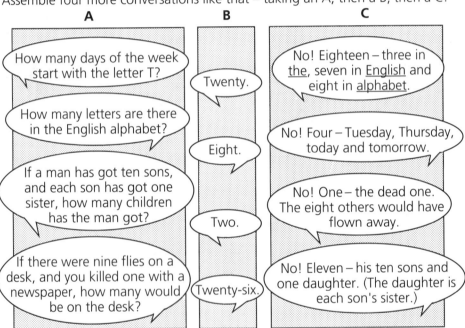

A

How many days of the week start with the letter T?

How many letters are there in the English alphabet?

If a man has got ten sons, and each son has got one sister, how many children has the man got?

If there were nine flies on a desk, and you killed one with a newspaper, how many would be on the desk?

B

Twenty.

Eight.

Two.

Twenty-six.

C

No! Eighteen – three in _the_, seven in _English_ and eight in _alphabet_.

No! Four – Tuesday, Thursday, today and tomorrow.

No! One – the dead one. The eight others would have flown away.

No! Eleven – his ten sons and one daughter. (The daughter is each son's sister.)

And here are four more trick questions. Perhaps you think the answer to each one is 'You can't do it. It's impossible' – but in fact each one has an answer. Think about each one for a few moments before you turn to the Solutions.

1) How can you jump from a twenty-metre ladder without hurting yourself?

2) How can you knock over a full glass without spilling any water?

3) How can you drop an egg six metres without breaking its shell?

4) How can you eat an egg without breaking its shell?

Find the endings

In each group in the grid, all three words need the same three letters at the end. Decide what the letters are, and write them in.

Then, for each group of words, find the correct group of pictures, and write the numbers in the correct boxes.

6
3	B	O	A	T
1	C	O	A	T
2	G	O	A	T

	B		
	C		
	H		

	B		
	H		
	P		

	B		
	H		
	W		

		T	
		D	
	H	E	

		C	
		L	
	S	N	

	C	L	
		L	
		S	

		D	
		G	
	P	L	

	H		
	N		
	R		

		H	
		P	
	W	H	

	L		
	N		
	W		

		M	
		N	
	S	P	

1

2

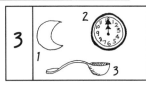
3

4

5

6

7

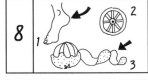
8

9

10

11

12

School crossword

The clues for this crossword are jokes. In each joke a teacher is talking to a student, and each joke takes place in a different lesson.

Take the letters *in italics* and put them into the correct order. They will spell the subjects of the lessons. Write the subjects in the grid.

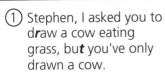

① Stephen, I asked you to d*r*aw a cow eating grass, bu*t* you've only drawn a cow.
 – Yes. The cow's eaten all the gr*a*ss.

② E*mm*a, if I cut *t*wo apple*s* in*t*o ten pi*e*ces and two pe*a*rs into ten pi*e*ces, what would I *h*ave?
 – A fru*i*t sal*a*d.

③ P*e*ggy, what can *y*ou tell m*e* about th*e* Dead Sea?
 – Nothing *r*eally. I didn't even know it w*a*s ill.

④ Rebe*cc*a, give me the *n*ame of a l*i*quid that won't fr*e*eze.
 – Boiling wat*e*r, *s*ir?

⑤ Edward, you've writt*e*n 'rabbit' w*i*th two Ts at the end. There *s*hou*l*d only be o*n*e.
 – Whic*h* T is the wron*g* one?

⑥ G*r*aham, wh*a*t is th*e* opposite of 'Nei*n*'?
 – Six?

⑦ Who can tell me *s*ome*th*ing impo*r*tant tha*t* didn't ex*i*st a hund*r*ed *y*ears ago?
 – Me!

Question:

What is the short form of Subject 2?

English Puzzles 3   Heinemann Internatic

Portable phone

Use these ten verbs, in their *-ing* form, to complete the sentences.
Then put the *-ing* forms into the grid.

attack   dance   look   pack   paint   pour

sculpt   smoke   test   train

1 Marco Polo was _____ his bags, when his portable phone rang.

2 Sherlock Holmes was _____ for his hat, when his portable phone rang.

3 Fred Astaire was _____ with Ginger Rogers, when his portable phone rang.

4 Robin Hood was _____ a castle, when his portable phone rang.

5 Daley Thompson was _____ for the Olympics, when his portable phone rang.

6 Leonardo da Vinci was _____ the 'Mona Lisa', when his portable phone rang.

7 Rodin was _____ the 'Thinker', when his portable phone rang.

8 Winston Churchill was _____ a cigar, when his portable phone rang.

9 William Shakespeare was _____ a glass of beer, when his portable phone rang.

10 George Michael was _____ a microphone, when his portable phone rang.

Question:

The letters in the special squares – ☐ – should spell the name of a tense (the tense used in the first part of each sentence in the puzzle). Which tense is it?

How old are they?

First, work out the age of each person. Then do the second part of the puzzle.

A
Born:
May 15. 2012

B
Born:
Dec. 14. 1988

C
Born:
Mar. 4. 2018

D
Born:
Aug. 10. 2034

E
Born:
Jun. 17. 1975

F
Born:
Oct. 8. 2011

G
Born:
Apr. 28. 2017

H
Born:
Jul. 2. 2004

I
Born:
Feb. 3. 2029

A	37	F	
B		G	
C		H	
D		I	
E		J	

J
Born:
Jan. 29. 2005

Which person does each of these sentences describe?
Write the correct letters.

☐ She's in her teens.		☐ She's in her late thirties.	
☐ He's nearly twenty-one.		☐ She's in her mid-forties.	
☐ He's in his early thirties.		☐ He's in his mid-forties.	
☐ She's in her early thirties.		☐ She's sixtyish.	
☐ He's in his late thirties.		☐ He's about seventy-five.	

A WALL OF WORDS

In each line of four words, one word is different from the other three. Which word is it, and why is it different?

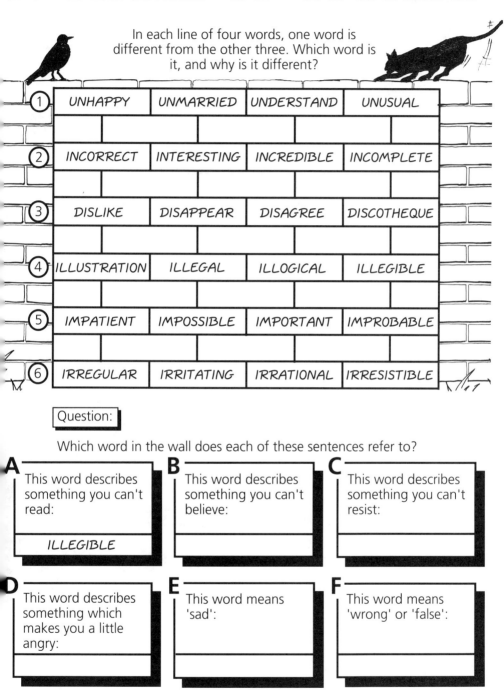

1	UNHAPPY	UNMARRIED	UNDERSTAND	UNUSUAL
2	INCORRECT	INTERESTING	INCREDIBLE	INCOMPLETE
3	DISLIKE	DISAPPEAR	DISAGREE	DISCOTHEQUE
4	ILLUSTRATION	ILLEGAL	ILLOGICAL	ILLEGIBLE
5	IMPATIENT	IMPOSSIBLE	IMPORTANT	IMPROBABLE
6	IRREGULAR	IRRITATING	IRRATIONAL	IRRESISTIBLE

Question:

Which word in the wall does each of these sentences refer to?

A This word describes something you can't read:

ILLEGIBLE

B This word describes something you can't believe:

C This word describes something you can't resist:

D This word describes something which makes you a little angry:

E This word means 'sad':

F This word means 'wrong' or 'false':

TOOLBOX

Put the letters for each tool in the correct order, and
write the words in the correct places.

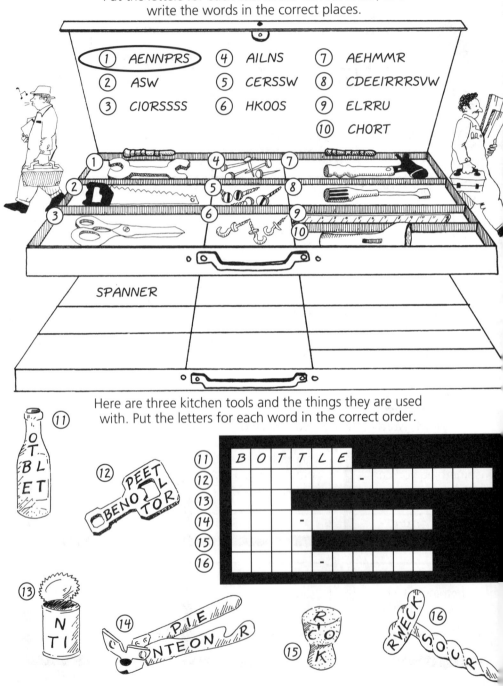

① AENNPRS   ④ AILNS   ⑦ AEHMMR
② ASW   ⑤ CERSSW ⑧ CDEEIRRRSVW
③ CIORSSSS ⑥ HKOOS   ⑨ ELRRU
                      ⑩ CHORT

SPANNER

Here are three kitchen tools and the things they are used
with. Put the letters for each word in the correct order.

⑪ OT BL ET

⑫ PEET BENO L TOR

⑬ N TI

⑭ PIE NTEON R

⑮ R CO K

⑯ RWECK SOUR

⑪	B	O	T	T	L	E							
⑫							-					
⑬												
⑭					-						
⑮											
⑯					-					

COMPUTER ERROR!

There is a computer error in each of the eight sentences. In the first one, for example, the computer has printed P instead of L. Correct the sentences, and then put them in the pictures.

> SHAPP I CAPP A DOCTOR?
> SHALL I BPEN THE DBBR FBR YBU?
> CET'S GO FOR A WACK.
> I'LL CUD DHE DOMADOES – YOU WASH DHE LEDDUCE.
> SHYLL WE TYKE Y TYXI?
> WHY DON'T WU GO TO THU CINUMA THIS UVUNING?
> WFERE SFALL I PUT TFIS CFAIR?
> KHO SHALL KE INVITE TO THE KEDDING?

1

2

3

4

5

SHALL I CALL A DOCTOR?

6

7

8

THE LAST WORD

Look at these five book titles (the books are all by the English writer Ivy Compton-Burnett):

Ivy Compton-Burnett	BROTHERS AND SISTERS
Ivy Compton-Burnett	PARENTS AND CHILDREN
Ivy Compton-Burnett	THE LAST AND THE FIRST
Ivy Compton-Burnett	THE PRESENT AND THE PAST
Ivy Compton-Burnett	MOTHER AND SON

As you can see, each title is a 'pair' of expressions.

Here are fifteen books by other writers, from the United Kingdom, Ireland, the United States and Canada. Each title is a 'pair' of expressions. Can you work out the last word of each one? (All the words you need are at the bottom of the page.)

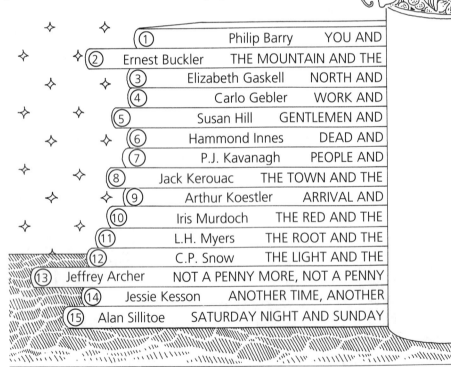

1	Philip Barry	YOU AND
2	Ernest Buckler	THE MOUNTAIN AND THE
3	Elizabeth Gaskell	NORTH AND
4	Carlo Gebler	WORK AND
5	Susan Hill	GENTLEMEN AND
6	Hammond Innes	DEAD AND
7	P.J. Kavanagh	PEOPLE AND
8	Jack Kerouac	THE TOWN AND THE
9	Arthur Koestler	ARRIVAL AND
10	Iris Murdoch	THE RED AND THE
11	L.H. Myers	THE ROOT AND THE
12	C.P. Snow	THE LIGHT AND THE
13	Jeffrey Archer	NOT A PENNY MORE, NOT A PENNY
14	Jessie Kesson	ANOTHER TIME, ANOTHER
15	Alan Sillitoe	SATURDAY NIGHT AND SUNDAY

ALIVE   CITY   DARK   DEPARTURE   FLOWER   GREEN   I   LADIES
LESS   MORNING   PLACE   PLAY   PLACES   SOUTH   VALLEY

English Puzzles 3   Heinemann International

SOLUTIONS

PUZZLE 1   Down the steps

1 Could you carry this for me, please?
2 Could you cash these travellers cheques, please?
3 Could you pass me that hammer, please?
4 Could you sign at the bottom, please?
5 Could you come back tomorrow morning, please?
6 Could you wait just a moment, please?
7 Could you turn down the TV, please?

PUZZLE 2   Electrical appliances

	a	b	c	d	e	f	g	h	i	j	k	l	m	n	o	p	q
1	V	A	C	U	U	M	–	C	L	E	A	N	E	R			
2	W	A	S	H	I	N	G	–	M	A	C	H	I	N	E		
3	R	E	F	R	I	G	E	R	A	T	O	R					
4	D	I	S	H	W	A	S	H	E	R							
5	C	O	M	P	U	T	E	R									
6	C	A	S	S	E	T	T	E	–	P	L	A	Y	E	R		
7	T	Y	P	E	W	R	I	T	E	R							
8	C	O	F	F	E	E	–	M	A	K	E	R					
9	A	N	S	W	E	R	I	N	G	–	M	A	C	H	I	N	E
10	V	I	D	E	O	–	R	E	C	O	R	D	E	R			

9m	3k	5c	6j	1b	8a	7h		10c	2e	4g	1h		5d	1i	4f	6m	3g	9f
C	O	M	P	A	C	T		D	I	S	C		P	L	A	Y	E	R

Remember: People often say *fridge* instead of *refrigerator*, and *video* instead of *video-recorder*.

PUZZLE 3   Unusual activities

1 He's going to walk a mile on his hands.
2 He's going to stand on one leg in a bucket of soup for twenty-four hours.
3 She's going to play the trumpet non-stop for twenty-four hours.
4 She's going to run a marathon with an egg balanced on a spoon.
5 She's going to juggle three oranges and an apple for twenty-four hours.
6 He's going to take as many showers as possible in four hours.
7 She's going to throw five hundred balls through a tyre.
8 He's going to walk up and down a ladder with a frying-pan on his head.

PUZZLE 4   Find the beginnings

7 2 CHAIR 3 CHEESE 1 CHURCH
1 3 SKIRT 1 SKATE 2 SKIER
6 2 STAMP 3 STEAK 1 STAR

10 1 SPOON 3 SPIDER 2 SPIRAL
3 3 SHIRT 2 SHOES 1 SHEEP
11 2 FLAG 1 FLUTE 3 FLOWER

8 2 FROG 1 FRUIT 3 FRIDGE
4 1 BREAD 2 BRICK 3 BRUSH
2 2 TRAY 3 TREE 1 TRAIN

5 2 DRUMS 3 DRESS 1 DRAWER
12 1 PLUG 2 PLANT 3 PLATE
9 2 CLOUD 1 CLOCK 3 CLIFF

PUZZLE 5   Rhyming pairs

EYE – TIE, SQUARE – PEAR, SNAKE – STEAK, TAIL – WHALE, DRUM – THUMB, WHEEL – MEAL, WOOL – BULL, CHEQUE – NECK, KEY – KNEE, FIRE – TYRE

Note: The spellings 'cheque' and 'tyre' are British English. In American English, the spellings are 'check' and 'tire'.

PUZZLE 6   Sorry – I can explain!

1 I'm sorry I didn't phone you. I lost your number.
2 I'm sorry I didn't recognise you. I'm not wearing my glasses.
3 I'm sorry I forgot your birthday. I thought it was the seventeenth, not the seventh.
4 I'm sorry I didn't come to your party on Saturday. I was working all weekend.
5 I'm sorry I didn't finish typing your letters. The typewriter broke down.

PUZZLE 7   Parts of the body

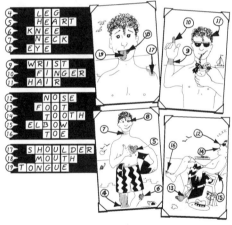

4 LEG
5 HEART
6 KNEE
7 NECK
8 EYE
9 WRIST
10 FINGER
11 HAIR
12 NOSE
13 FOOT
14 TOOTH
15 ELBOW
16 TOE
17 SHOULDER
18 MOUTH
19 TONGUE

Answers to questions:
– The plural of Number 13, *foot*, is *feet*; the plural of Number 14, *tooth*, is *teeth*.
– In Number 6, *knee*, the *k* is not pronounced; in Number 9, *wrist*, the *w* is not pronounced.

PUZZLE 8   Elephant jokes

1 How does an elephant get down from a tree? – It sits on a leaf and waits for autumn.
2 How do you put an elephant in a matchbox? – You take the matches out first.
3 What time is it when an elephant sits on a chair? – It's time to get a new chair.
4 How do you know if an elephant has been in your fridge? – You can see footprints in the butter.
5 Can an elephant jump higher than a lamp-post? – Yes. Lamp-posts can't jump.
6 How do you get four elephants into a car? – You put two in the front and two in the back.
7 How do you know if there's an elephant under your bed? – The ceiling is very close.

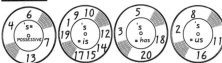

PUZZLE 9   Jukebox

Note: The contraction 's only means us in the expression Let's... (songs 2,8,11,16). The complete form, Let us..., is very rarely used.

PUZZLE 10   Who are the others?

one, fourteen, 1, 14, CHARLES DE GAULLE
two, ten, eighteen, 2, 10, 18, CHARLIE CHAPLIN
three, eleven, 3, 11, JAMES BOND
four, nine, twenty, 4, 9, 20, LUDWIG VAN BEETHOVEN
five, sixteen, nineteen, 5, 16, 19, LEONARDO DA VINCI
six, thirteen, 6, 13, BUFFALO BILL
seven, twelve, seventeen, 7, 12, 17, SHERLOCK HOLMES
eight, fifteen, 8, 15, WALT DISNEY

Answer to question: James Bond and Sherlock Holmes are not real people.

PUZZLE 11   Verb flags

1 come, came, come.   6 dance, danced, danced.
2 swim, swam, swum.   7 put, put, put.
3 study, studied, studied.   8 stop, stopped, stopped.
4 wait, waited, waited.   9 read, read, read.
5 be, was/were, been.

Answers to questions:
– The verbs on these flags 🏳 are irregular verbs, and the verbs on these flags 🏳 are regular verbs.
– A:6. B:3. C:9. D:5. E:2. F:8. G:1. H:7. I:4.

PUZZLE 12   Eight proverbs

1 People who live in glass houses shouldn't throw stones.
2 The first step is the hardest.
3 Walls have ears.
4 When the cat's away, the mice will play.
5 Time is money.
6 While there's life, there's hope.
7 Sleep is better than medicine.
8 The grass is always greener on the other side of the fence.

PUZZLE 13   Album tracks

Side A		Side B	
1	Bad	1	Another part of me
2	The way you make me feel	2	Man in the mirror
3	Speed demon	3	I just can't stop loving you
4	Liberian girl	4	Dirty Diana
5	Just good friends	5	Smooth criminal

PUZZLE 14   From dinosaurs to dynamite

1 = G   3 = A   5 = C   7 = E   8 = F
2 = D   4 = H   6 = B

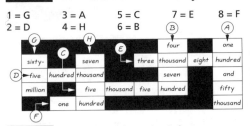

PUZZLE 15   Complete the jokes

1 T If I had eight oranges in my right hand and ten oranges in my left hand, what would I have?
   S Very big hands.

2 T If you had fifty dollars in one jacket-pocket and a hundred dollars in another jacket-pocket, what would you have?
   S Someone else's jacket.

3 T If I offered you eight hamburgers or eighty hamburgers, which would you prefer?
   S Eight.
   T Eight? Don't you know the difference between eight and eighty?
   S Yes, but I don't like hamburgers.

4 T If I had ten apples in each pocket of my trousers, what would I have?
   S Very heavy trousers.

5 T If I gave you three rabbits today and five rabbits tomorrow, how many rabbits would you have?
   S Nine.
   T Nine?
   S Yes. I've already got one at home.

6 T If I said 'What is the plural of "mouse"?', what would you say?
   S Mice.
   T And if I said 'What is the plural of "baby"?', what would you say?
   S Twins.

Words including the letter **N** are placed at *North*; words including the letters **NW** are placed at *North West*; words including the letter **S** are placed at *South*; words including the letters **SE** are placed at *South East*, etc.

North: PANDA, PAINT, BALCONY.
North East: NET, NECK.
East: CAMERA, LADDER, COMPUTER.
South East: CASE, MUSEUM, HORSE.
South: SHIP, SCARF, TOURIST, LIPSTICK.
South West: SWITCH.
West: WATCH, COW, WOOD.
North West: RUNWAY.

PUZZLE 17   Five pockets

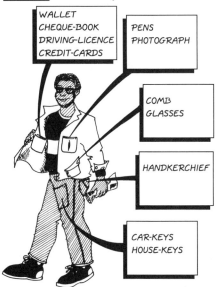

WALLET
CHEQUE-BOOK
DRIVING-LICENCE
CREDIT-CARDS

PENS
PHOTOGRAPH

COMB
GLASSES

HANDKERCHIEF

CAR-KEYS
HOUSE-KEYS

Note: In American English, *driver's license* is used instead of *driving-licence*.

PUZZLE 18   It doesn't rhyme!

PUZZLE 19   Reveal the answers

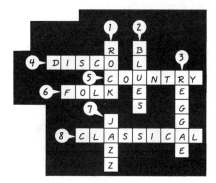

Remember:
Most adjectives become adverbs by adding *-ly*: badly, carefully, clearly, correctly, politely, quickly, slowly.
Adjectives ending *-le* change this ending to *-ly*: gentle – gently.
Adjectives ending *-y* change this ending to *-ily*: angry – angrily, easy – easily, happy – happily.
For the adjective *good*, the adverb is *well*.

PUZZLE 20   Riddles

1 A hole.
2 A stamp.
3 A blackboard.
4 Rain.
5 A telephone.
6 A comb.
7 A hot dog.
8 A mushroom.

PUZZLE 21   Guitar chords

PUZZLE 22   Looking into the future

1 We will never go to the moon.
2 In the twentieth century, war will not exist.
3 The Rolling Stones will only be popular for two years.
4 They will never do it. It's impossible.
5 Fidel Castro will not be president for more than a year.
6 The world will end on 20th February, 1524.

PUZZLE 23 Waiter!

1	BREAD	5	MILK	9	SPIDER
2	COFFEE	6	PIZZA	10	TEA
3	FLY	7	SOAP	11	THUMB
4	ICE-CREAM	8	SOUP		

Waiter! There's a fly in my soup! – Don't worry, sir. The spider on your bread will kill it.

Waiter! What's this fly doing in my soup? – I think it's swimming , sir.

Waiter! What's this fly doing on my ice-cream? – I think it's learning to ski, sir.

Waiter! Your thumb is in my soup! – Don't worry, sir. It's not very hot.

Waiter! I'll have coffee without milk, please. – We haven't got any milk sir. Would you like coffee without cream?

Waiter! This coffee tastes like soap! – Ah, that must be tea, sir. The coffee tastes like glue.

Waiter! How long will my pizza be? – It won't be *long*, sir. It'll be *round*.

PUZZLE 24 Words into numbers

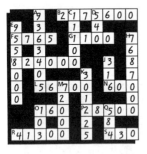

PUZZLE 25 At the cinema

1 WAR FILM

2 WESTERN

3 CARTOON

4 HORROR FILM

5 SCIENCE FICTION FILM

6 COMEDY

PUZZLE 26 Heavy syllables

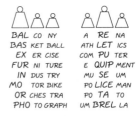

BAL co NY
BAS KET BALL
EX er CISE
FUR NI TURE
IN DUS TRY
MO TOR BIKE
OR CHES TRA
PHO TO GRAPH

A RE NA
ATH LET ICS
COM PU TER
E QUIP MENT
MU SE UM
PO LICE MAN
PO TA TO
UM BREL LA

PUZZLE 27 Special sentences

In Sentence 9, all the words except one include double letters.
In Sentence 7, four words begin with the same letter.
In Sentence 5, all the words have the same number of letters.
In Sentence 4, all the words begin with the same letter.
In Sentence 8, the second word has one more letter than the first word, the third word has one more letter than the second word, and so on.
In Sentence 3, only one word includes the letter *e*.
In Sentence 10, there is a consonant, then a vowel, then a consonant, then a vowel, and so on.
In Sentence 6, three words include the letter *v*.
In Sentence 2, the letters are an anagram of *Warm feet, Beethoven?*

Answers to questions:
– The tense in all ten sentences is the *Present Perfect*.
–You can contract *has* to *'s*: *Tom's broken his arm, Helen's hurt her hand, Jo's made seven albums, Bill's written three books.*
You can contract *have* to *'ve*: *We've visited five countries, We've gone home!*

PUZZLE 28 Find the middles

5	2 SALT
	1 BALL
	3 HALF

6	2 BUTTER
	3 BOTTLE
	1 LETTER

3	1 HONEY
	3 CONES
	2 MONEY

7	3 DOOR
	2 POOL
	1 FOOT

1	1 BUTCHER
	3 MATCHES
	2 KITCHEN

9	2 NAIL
	3 HAIR
	1 RAIN

2	2 EIGHT
	1 LIGHT
	3 NIGHT

8	2 COLLAR
	1 WALLET
	3 PILLOW

4	2 FIRE
	3 GIRL
	1 BIRD

PUZZLE 29   Doctor!

1 Use a pen.
2 When did *what* happen?
3 I know, doctor. I've been ill.
4 Well, you've got it again.
5 I'm nervous too. It's the first operation I've ever done.
6 Who said that?
7 That's fantastic! I've never been able to play it before.
8 Next!

PUZZLE 30   Numberplates

①	M	I	R	R	O	R					
②	H	E	A	D	L	I	G	H	T	S	
③	W	I	N	D	S	C	R	E	E	N	
④	S	T	E	E	R	I	N	G	-	W	H	E	E	L
⑤	B	O	N	N	E	T					
⑥	E	N	G	I	N	E					
⑦	S	E	A	T	B	E	L	T			
⑧	B	U	M	P	E	R					

Note: In American English, *license plate* is used instead of *numberplate*; also, *windshield* is used instead of *windscreen*, and *hood* instead of *bonnet*.

PUZZLE 31   Absurd riddles

1 A tomato in a lift.
2 A man on a horse.
3 An omelette in a washing machine.
4 A penguin on rollerskates.
5 A zebra with a trumpet.
6 A bird in a submarine.
7 A rabbit on a motorbike.
8 A giraffe with a microphone.

The answer to the question *What is big and yellow and eats rocks?* is *A big yellow rock-eater.*

PUZZLE 32   Crossword in two halves

Part A   Part B

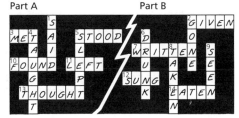

All the verbs are irregular, but:
- for the verbs in Part A, the Past Simple and the Past Participle are the same: meet/*met*/*met*, say/*said*/*said*, stand/*stood*/*stood*, etc.;
- for the verbs in Part B, the Past Simple and the Past Participle are different: give/*gave*/*given*, go/*went*/*gone*, write/*wrote*/*written*, etc.

PUZZLE 33   Film encyclopedia

1 THE MAN WHO CAME TO DINNER.
2 THE MAN WITH THE GOLDEN GUN.
3 THE MAN FROM LARAMIE.
4 THE MAN ON THE EIFFEL TOWER.
5 THE MAN WHO WATCHED TRAINS GO BY.
6 THE MAN IN THE BACK SEAT.
7 THE MAN WHO SHOT LIBERTY VALANCE.
8 THE MAN IN THE WHITE SUIT.

Answer to question:
The hidden word in each title is *who*: THE BOY WHO STOLE A MILLION, THE GIRL WHO HAD EVERYTHING, THE SPY WHO LOVED ME, THE WOMAN WHO CAME BACK.

PUZZLE 34   Silent letters

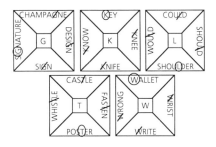

1 B	4 K	7 B	10 K	12 W
2 K	5 T	8 B	11 W	13 L
3 T	6 B	9 G		

Remember these useful rules:
- In *-mb* at the end of a word, the *b* is always silent.
- In *-gn* or *-gne* at the end of a word, the *g* is always silent.
- In *kn-* at the beginning of a word, the *k* is always silent.
- In *wr-* at the beginning of a word, the *w* is always silent.
- In *could, should* and *would*, the *l* is always silent.
- In *-st-* in the middle of a word, the *t* is usually pronounced, but it is silent in some words.

PUZZLE 35   Football team

PUZZLE 36   Personality

1 LAZY   2 GENEROUS
3 BOSSY   4 FRIENDLY
5 BAD-TEMPERED   6 PATIENT
7 DISHONEST   8 EASY-GOING

Answer to question:
The people in the first group have bad qualities (*lazy, bossy, bad-tempered* and *dishonest*); the people in the second group have good qualities (*generous, friendly, patient* and *easy-going*).

If you are interested in cards, you may like to know these English words:

A = Ace   ◇ = Diamonds
J = Jack   ♡ = Hearts
Q = Queen   ♣ = Clubs
K = King   ♠ = Spades

So this card is the [A ◇] This card is the [2 ♡]
Ace of Diamonds: Two of Hearts: etc.

PUZZLE 37   Past, present and future

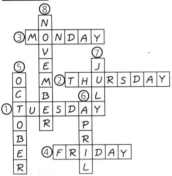

PUZZLE 38   A strange quiz

1 The letter L.
2 Because it changes ice into mice.
3 How do you pronounce 'y-e-s'?
4 Are you asleep?
5 Smiles (because there is a mile between the first letter and the last letter).
6 The word that's spelt w-r-o-n-g-l-y.
7 Sixty.
8 The letter R.
9 The letters M and I.
10 Post office.
11 Because it makes oil boil.
12 Because it's always in bed.
13 Because it's in the middle of water.

PUZZLE 39   Which routes ?

1 C → E   4 A → H
2 J → G   5 E → J
3 H → D   6 B → F

PUZZLE 40   Department store

Ground floor	1	BOOKS
	2	TOYS
	3	RECORDS
	4	STATIONERY
First floor	1	FURNITURE
	2	SHOES
	3	ELECTRICAL APPLIANCES
Second floor	1	MEN'S CLOTHING
	2	WOMEN'S CLOTHING
	3	PHOTOGRAPHIC EQUIPMENT

Did you remember to put an apostrophe in *MEN'S* and in *WOMEN'S*?

PUZZLE 41   Missing words

They've been married *for* forty years.
We've only lived in this house *for* a week.
I've been here *since* six o'clock.
We've known each other *for* ages!
Zambia has been independent *since* 1964.
I've had this car *for* twenty-five years.
We've been away *for* six months.
I've been here *for* twenty minutes.
He's been interested in horses *since* he was a boy.
She's worked in this office *for* thirty years.

The tense is the *Present Perfect*. This tense is used in all the sentences in the pictures.

PUZZLE 42   Trick questions

– How many days of the week start with the letter T?
– Two.
– No! Four – Tuesday, Thursday, today and tomorrow.

– How many letters are there in the English alphabet?
– Twenty-six.
– No! Eighteen – three in *the*, seven in *English* and eight in *alphabet*.

– If a man has got ten sons, and each son has got one sister, how many children has the man got?
– Twenty.
– No! Eleven – his ten sons and one daughter. (The daughter is each son's sister.)

– If there were nine flies on a desk, and you killed one with a newspaper, how many would be on the desk?
– Eight.
– No! One – the dead one. The eight others would have flown away.

1 Jump from near the bottom.
2 Knock over a glass of milk.
3 Drop it seven metres. (For the first six metres, it will be unbroken.)
4 Ask someone else to break the shell.

PUZZLE 43   Find the endings

6 — 3 BOAT / 1 COAT / 2 GOAT
9 — 3 TART / 1 DART / 2 HEART
5 — 3 HOSE / 1 NOSE / 2 ROSE
4 — 2 BOOK / 3 COOK / 1 HOOK
7 — 2 CAKE / 3 LAKE / 1 SNAKE
8 — 1 HEEL / 3 PEEL / 2 WHEEL
11 — 1 BILL / 3 HILL / 2 PILL
2 — 3 CLOCK / 2 LOCK / 1 SOCK
10 — 3 LINE / 1 NINE / 2 WINE
1 — 2 BALL / 3 HALL / 1 WALL
12 — 3 DATE / 2 GATE / 1 PLATE
3 — 1 MOON / 2 NOON / 3 SPOON

PUZZLE 44   School crossword

1 ART
2 MATHEMATICS
3 GEOGRAPHY
4 SCIENCE
5 ENGLISH
6 GERMAN
7 HISTORY

The short form of *mathematics* is *maths* in British English and *math* in American English.

PUZZLE 45   Portable phone

Remember:
Verbs ending with a consonant + e lose the e when adding *-ing*:
dance – dancing,
smoke – smoking.

Answer to question: The tense in the first part of each sentence is the *Past Continuous*.

PUZZLE 46   How old are they?

A	37	D	She's in her teens.
B	61	I	He's nearly twenty-one.
C	31	G	He's in his early thirties.
D	15	C	She's in her early thirties.
E	74	F	He's in his late thirties.
F	38	A	She's in her late thirties.
G	32	J	She's in her mid-forties.
H	45	H	He's in his mid-forties.
I	20	B	She's sixtyish.
J	44	E	He's about seventy-five.

Note: The ending *-ish* is very useful. As you can see from *sixtyish* ('about sixty'), it has the idea of 'approximately'. Here are some more examples: *smallish* ('quite small, but not very small'), *youngish* ('quite young, but not very young'), *greenish* ('not exactly green, but more like green than another colour').

PUZZLE 47   A wall of words

These are the 'different' words:
1 UNDERSTAND.
2 INTERESTING.
3 DISCOTHEQUE.
4 ILLUSTRATION.
5 IMPORTANT.
6 IRRITATING.

They are different from the others because you can't take away their beginnings (UN-, IN-, DIS-, IL-, IM-, IR-).

In the other words, each beginning is a negative prefix. You can take it away and find the opposite of the word:
UNHAPPY – HAPPY, UNMARRIED – MARRIED, UNUSUAL – USUAL, INCORRECT – CORRECT, etc.

Answer to question:
A ILLEGIBLE   D IRRITATING
B INCREDIBLE   E UNHAPPY
C IRRESISTIBLE   F INCORRECT

PUZZLE 48   Toolbox

11 BOTTLE
12 BOTTLE-OPENER
13 TIN
14 TIN-OPENER
15 CORK
16 CORK-SCREW

PUZZLE 49   Computer error!

1 I'll cut the tomatoes - you wash the lettuce.
2 Who shall we invite to the wedding?
3 Shall I open the door for you?
4 Why don't we go to the cinema this evening?
5 Shall I call a doctor?
6 Shall we take a taxi?
7 Where shall I put this chair?
8 Let's go for a walk.

PUZZLE 50   The last word

1 YOU AND I
2 THE MOUNTAIN AND THE VALLEY
3 NORTH AND SOUTH
4 WORK AND PLAY
5 GENTLEMEN AND LADIES
6 DEAD AND ALIVE
7 PEOPLE AND PLACES
8 THE TOWN AND THE CITY
9 ARRIVAL AND DEPARTURE
10 THE RED AND THE GREEN
11 THE ROOT AND THE FLOWER
12 THE LIGHT AND THE DARK
13 NOT A PENNY MORE, NOT A PENNY LESS
14 ANOTHER TIME, ANOTHER PLACE
15 SATURDAY NIGHT AND SUNDAY MORNING

Index

If you want to do puzzles about particular points, you can find them in this Index. For example, if you want to do a puzzle about adjectives of personality, do Puzzle 36.